Southern Steam Days Remembered IV

Strathwood

RAILWAY WORLD

Railway Magazine

Loco-Shed BOOK

abc

SHED ALLOCATIONS OF ALL BRITISH RAILWAY LOCOMOTIVES

BRITISH RAILWAYS

PASSENGER SERVICES

LONDON

Victoria   London Bridge
Waterloo   Cannon Street
Charing Cross   Holborn Viaduct

SOUTH AND WEST OF ENGLAND
(Including Suburban Services)

SEPTEMBER 25th, 1950
until further notice

ONE SHILLING

BRITISH RAILWAYS
STEAM LOCOMOTIVES
Western & Southern

IAN ALLAN
a b c

TEMPLECOMBE

Southern Steam Days Remembered IV

Front Cover: One of earlier members of the Merchant Navy Class to be rebuilt was 35016 Elders Fyffes in April 1957, we see her towards the close of the following year passing Winchfield with the down Bournemouth Belle on 14 December 1958. *Colour Rail*

Strathwood

Southern Steam Days Remembered IV

A selection of some of the essential books and magazines from the era along with a few other reminders of the locomotives.

First published 2019

ISBN 978-1-913390-05-1

Copyright Strathwood Publishing 2019
Published by Strathwood Publishing, 9 Boswell Crescent, Inverness, IV2 3ET
Telephone 01463 234004
Printed by Akcent Media

Contents

Preface... 6

Introduction - One of those Days.. 7

Back to School Days.. 11

Branches & Byways.. 24

Names of Distinction... 55

Southern Specials... 65

Sheds & Works Visits... 83

Isle of Wight Sunset... 114

Through the Links.. 124

Preface

We have often been asked to encourage another of my old friends from Western Australia, Roger Carrell to come up with some further reminiscences from his firing days based out of 70A Nine Elms. Once again Roger has not let us down as he takes us back to the early sixties and the still mainly steam run Southern Region for another helping for us all to enjoy.

We will all have our favourites from the past, I hope you will enjoy this compilation and we must also thank the foresight of the photographers and the kindness of those who have allowed their work to be seen and appreciated by a wider audience too.

Kevin Derrick
Inverness 2019

One old hand makes his way off duty towards the station here at Bournemouth on 28 May 1966, meanwhile, his workmates appear to be busy attending to the shed's rather basic coaling facilities. *Terry Tacey/The Transport Treasury*

Introduction - One of those Days

My driver, Harold Dory, and I had booked-on late-morning on a blustery autumn day to work a semi-fast, ex-Salisbury, from Basingstoke to Waterloo. We boarded 73081 Excalibur on the Up Through platform and, after some handover pleasantries with the Salisbury crew and a right-away from the guard, we departed - onto the Up Local and all stations to Woking thence non-stop to Waterloo.

The journey was uneventful until we got to Sturt Lane Junction, just past Farnborough, whereupon my firing shovel broke in two and upon arrival at the next station - Brookwood - I walked back along our train towards our guard with the blade of my shovel in one hand and the wooden handle in the other (much to the cackling of two old ladies), to ask if he carried a spare or two!

That resulted in a blank look from him accompanied by meek apologies regarding my predicament (while trying not to laugh!). A porter was summoned and following a brief disappearance, he re-emerged proudly brandishing the station master's garden spade. I gratefully accepted this - surely, anything to avoid throwing coal in by hand was an advantage. As it turned out, I got nowhere with the garden spade and throwing lumps of coal into the firebox by hand was becoming a bit blistery upon flesh, so I got the best results by simply using the blade of my firing shovel!

We arrived at Waterloo on time and upon release, we ran light to Nine Elms Loco and abandoned Excalibur to a 70A crew on prep. & disposal duties. There had been no comment regarding the shovel (or spade) which must have been regarded as just another hazard of the job. A visit to the running foreman's office gave us 34026 Yes Tor (a Rebuilt Bulleid Pacific) to prepare and work the 15:54 semi-fast to Salisbury back to Basing'.

Below: A filthy Standard Class 4MT from 70A Nine Elms has just a short while to go working as one of the last of the steam era pilots here at Waterloo in 1967. *Rail Online*

The usual filthy state of the footplate and lack of tools necessitated the now-accepted pursuit of raiding other engines for our quota. That done, a healthy fire was made-up, with the boiler water level maintained at three-quarters of a glass as the pressure rose. We had about an hour before departure, so I washed down the footplate while Harold went off to make a can of tea and we relaxed to eat our grub.

When 15:00 hours arrived we made our way to the nearest water column to fill the tender tank, thence onto the turntable which directed us onto the exit coal road. Following a full bunker of coal being taken and trimmed, we made our way sedately up to the exit dummy (disc signal) which sat atop a post. Having got the dummy, we chuffed our way up to the spur siding and awaited our path to Waterloo just before the shoppers' rush-hour was starting. I put the injector on with the tender sprays - to reduce dust - and ten minutes later we got the dummy to cross the Down Slow and achieve the Up Slow tender- first to Waterloo.

Arrival at Waterloo necessitated the usual routine of coupling up, exchanging disc boards from tender to smokebox - (one at the top and one at the bottom); check the smokebox door for tightness and removing our tail lamp. The guard had strolled up and was giving Harold the train's particulars - "Ten on, six Mk1s plus four GUVs", I overheard him say, an easy load for a 7P Pacific.

At 15:45 hrs I turned on the blower a little and pushed the dart into the fire to warm her up (and avoid too much smoke!). Just when the guard's whistle was heard, a figure appeared out of nowhere, struggling to gain access, in the form of a footplate inspector. Oh dear, I thought, what have I done to deserve this? He seemed friendly enough, didn't say a word to me but exchanged a few occasionally with Harold. What had *he* done, I wondered?

This train wasn't usually a substantial one - four plus a van being the usual load and this class of engine usually steamed on the smell of Anthracite, let alone the lumpy stuff itself! As we chuffed our way through Vauxhall, I was becoming a little concerned with steam pressure and the dullness of the fire.

By the time Harold shut off for the 40 mph curve at Clapham Junction, we were down from a working pressure of 280psi and the usual feathering at the safety valves, to

Left: This young fireman take his chance for a breather at Waterloo around 1963, as he already has a good fire showing within the firebox of 34090 Sir Eustace Missenden, Southern Railway as they await departure. *Colour Rail*

230psi, and had only gained 5psi by the time he opened her up again.

As we chattered up the hill, thence through Earlsfield, our guest was showing a growing interest in my steam pressure and water level, which was all I needed - a black mark on my personal file!

We made successful progress on the rising switchback through Wimbledon and onto Raynes Park after which the line levels out a bit through Berrylands, and even dips through Surbiton. But things got progressively worse and I was committed to using the pricker continuously in an attempt to clear the firebars and brighten the fire somewhat.

Approaching Hampton Court Junction we were definitely 'down-the-pan' and all Harold could do was ease her back to about 40 mph to hold steam pressure and avoid the brakes from going on. It was no surprise, therefore, that the Bobby there had us signalled from the Down Fast to the Down Local - to get us out of the way of the 16:00hrs West of England Express which must have been close to our heels by now.

By the time we limped into Woking - our first stop - we were in a very sorry state indeed. Our guest came over to me and asked to see the fire, so I opened the butterflies and introduced him to a 6 inch thick flat bed of glowing blue flames. "Nothing wrong with that is there!" was all he could say. Then he bid us farewell and departed.

Nothing wrong with that...? I trust he was referring to my efforts, not the fire! Anyway, the stop at Woking gave us opportunity to regain some steam pressure and half a glass of water. And, as we would be leap-frogging our way 'all

Left: Certainly the condition externally and perhaps internally too has very much gone downhill just a few years later in here at Waterloo with this view of 34021 Dartmoor in 1967. *Strathwood Library Collection*

stations' to Basing', some respectability might be maintained if not gained.

By the time we trundled into Basingstoke Station, twenty minutes late, I was wringing wet with sweat and filthy dirty. We happily handed our 'invalid' over to our Salisbury reliefs and, as a rough trip with a Bulleid Pacific was a rarity, we were left to assume we had been given a load of poor coal. The thirty-year old fireman sympathised with me, while convinced that he had the experience and know-how to recover the engine and gain some lost time.

We met up with our Salisbury colleagues about three weeks later and the driver, recognising us, came over and excitedly related that they had had a bugger of a time with the engine also, and upon taking her to shed for disposal, opened up the smokebox door to be confronted with a petticoat that had severed itself from the chimney and lay surrounding the blast pipe - thus, negating its ability as a venturi to create a vacuum in the smokebox and provide a draught to the fire!

It later dawned upon me that the presence of our footplate inspector may well have been in consequence to a complaint about the engine's inability to make steam. But the mystery remains why anyone, except an inexperienced passed cleaner, had not opened the smokebox door, (to remove char, etc.), and noticed that things were definitely amiss. I checked all smokeboxes, even Standard 'self-cleaning' ones, during preparations after that!

Roger Carrell - West Australia - 2017

Left: Bulleid's rebuilt Battle of Britain Pacific, 34109 Sir Trafford Leigh-Mallory blankets Basingstoke shed with smoke as they restart an up goods out of the yard in March 1964. *Rail Photoprints*

Back to School Days

An interesting array of rolling stock is being brought into Basingstoke by Maunsell's Schools Class, 30913 Christ's Hospital, soon after its transfer from the Eastern Section at 73G Ramsgate to the Western Section out of 70A Nine Elms which took place in May 1959. *Colour Rail*

The loss of work on the Kent coast routes towards the late fifties was the death sentence for these powerful 4-4-0s, with their numbers being reduced from forty locomotives at the start of 1961, to just twenty-five by the close of the year. None would survive in service after December 1962, a visit to Brighton on 22 August found 30929 Malvern still smartly attired, but now with less than four months to go. Brighton shed took a number of the Schools Class into care and put them to work on cross-country services along the coast to Bournemouth. On just one of these jobs on 9 September 1959, 30900 Eton stands at Bournemouth ready for the return working to Brighton. *Both: Colour Rail*

Twenty-one of the Schools were rebuilt by Bulleid to gain the benefit of improvements to their draughting, with the fitting of Lemaitre multiple-jet blast pipes and the larger diameter chimney. These are worn by 30921 Shrewsbury, which is seen here near Winchfield filling in time with a mid-morning stopper during September 1962. The full benefits of these modifications were certainly wasted by rostering these very powerful 4-4-0s on duties such as this. With an abundance of Bulleid's light Pacifics and increased deliveries of the new Standard designs, nineteen of the class remained with their original chimneys until the end. One of these was 30910 Merchant Taylors, seen peeking from the shadows at Waterloo on 6 April 1961, blowing off with 220psi showing in the gauge.
Both: Colour Rail

With a Hawksworth coach leading this rake from the Western Region tucked in behind the locomotive, 30906 Sherborne from 70A Nine Elms has been chosen to head this mid-winter excursion from West Drayton to Alton, seen near Guildford on 24 January 1959. *Colour Rail*

Opposite: Crisply turned out on 25 February 1962, 30926 Repton has found itself back on its old stomping ground once more as it stands outside the sheds at Ashford in preparation of working the last leg of the L.C.G.B. Kentish Venturer Railtour back to Charing Cross. *Colour Rail*

Two of the Schools Class found themselves paired for their last year in traffic with the much larger bogie tenders from redundant Lord Nelsons, one of these, 30912 Downside, was seen running fast through Berrylands in January 1962, the other one was 30921 Shrewsbury. *Colour Rail*

Opposite: On 6 August 1961, when seen departing Brighton, 30934 St. Lawrence would certainly lose marks for presentation after being one of the last of her class to come over from the Eastern Section to become a 70D Basingstoke engine a few weeks later. *Colour Rail*

In September 1962, 30921 Shrewsbury gets another run out with a Lord Nelson tender on a stopper near Winchfield. *Colour Rail*

Opposite: Climbing steadily running against adverse signals, 30926 Repton approaches Shortlands Junction in October 1958 with an express from the Kent coast. *Rail Photoprints*

Waiting for her chance to take her next passenger service away from Brighton in August 1962, 30923 Bradfield stands by the shed exit with a tender filled with some impressive lumps of coal for the fireman to break up. *Colour Rail*

Opposite: She might be fully coaled too, but there is very little work for the coal hammer here on board 30936 Cranleigh, as she has just started her duty for today at Ashford in September 1960. *Colour Rail*

Branches and Byways

Tunbridge Wells West was once a busy location with a rather grand station building and an engine shed conveniently situated alongside. The engine shed and the station saw a progressive rundown from 1963 into 1965 as services dwindled away. Just before this started take a real effect, we see a pair of Standard Class 4MTs in the station around 1963. When this somewhat smaller Standard Class 2MT was recorded at New Romney in July 1957, she was just three months into service. The last ten of these 2-6-2Ts to be built all went to either Ashford or Ramsgate from new. *Both: Colour Rail*

The optimism of the Southern Railway for traffic on the Allhallows branch had all since vanished for the Southern Region, when this view was taken at Stoke Junction Halt on 2 December 1961. With two days until final closure enthusiasts make up the passenger numbers to ride and photograph this Wainwright H Class. *Colour Rail*

26

The same locomotive had previously seen its branch line duties pulled from beneath it already elsewhere, as we see it working on the Hawkhurst branch making a stop at Horsmonden on 3 June the same year, with just nine days before closure, once again enthusiasts bolster the passenger numbers. *Colour Rail*

The picturesque branch from Three Bridges to East Grinstead attracted a good number of cameramen before its closure. The usual motive power before the DEMUs took over was by push/pull operation using the two-car rebuilt Maunsell sets from the late fifties. These were often powered by a suitably equipped Class M7, such as 30053 seen at Grange Road on 12 June 1960 during a brief shower. Other regulars to be seen would be H Class 0-4-4Ts, such as 31005 calling at Rowfant on 3 July 1963, unusually working push/pull mode bunker first today. *Both: Colour Rail*

If we ignored the unsightly oil depot behind our camera position, the station at Rowfant was quite charming in springtime as here on 26 May 1963, just as another H Class gets away with a Three Bridges to East Grinstead service.
Strathwood Library Collection

Opposite: Everyday life in sixties Surrey takes little notice of this Standard Class 4MT, 80145 hauling another of those Maunsell based push/pull sets high above them at Oxted on 27 April 1963. *Colour Rail*

Below and opposite: With a good load of four coaches for a single locomotive on the line, 32650 rolls into North Hayling on 15 June 1958. This 1876 built example of the A1X Class had spent the years from 1930 until 1937 as a resident on the Isle of Wight, before starting a sixteen years stint as one of the Lancing works shunters until 1953. We catch her opposite on another visit to North Hayling in 1961.
Photos: Colour Rail

Above: The staple motive power for the Hayling Island branch was the Stroudley A1X Class Terriers, or 'Rooters' as they were known in some circles. The raison d'etre for their retention was, of course, the severe weight restrictions applied to Langstone Bridge demonstrated by 32670 making its way across on 27 July 1963 with the 16.35 Havant to Hayling Island service.
Rail Photoprints

Perhaps something has just caught the eyes of the crossing keeper, as 32650 pops up once again as one of the regulars on the Hayling Island branch, with the 15.05 service from Havant here at Langston crossing on 8 July 1962. *Rail Photoprints*

The signalman has headed back to the sanctuary of his box after exchanging the tokens here at Cranleigh from the driver of Ivatt Class 2MT, 41301, still with a 75A Brighton shed plate but just transferred to 70C Guildford. Notice the two different colours of the awnings around 1965. *Colour Rail*

The 4 ½ mile-long Bentley to Bordon branch was generally a sleepy sort of place, aside from the occasional troop special heading for the military camp at Longmoor. With the branch's closure notices already posted for the 16 September 1957, a couple of fellow enthusiasts make one last pilgrimage the day beforehand here to Bordon to see this Class M7 performing as the branch engine. *Colour Rail*

Opposite: The secondary byway linking Alton with the mainline once again at Winchester, also familiarly known as the Mid-Hants sees some forces action too in May 1957, as Lord Nelson, 30862 Lord Collingwood is held with a troop train in Medstead & Four Marks station. We are approaching off the single line on the footplate of an M7 with a down Winchester local, just as the signalman waits to collect the tablet. *Colour Rail*

With a couple of ex-LSWR coaches bolstered up with a utility van, we see another of 71A Eastleigh's Class M7s, 30481 rounding the tight curve to reach the Southampton mainline at Winchester Junction after a light snowfall in March 1954. *Colour Rail*

Opposite: A similar combination but with more modern Maunsell stock throughout leaves the mainline behind at Lymington Junction on 27 July 1963, with one of 71B Bournemouth's Class M7s 30108 in charge. They head for Holmsley, Ringwood and West Moors on the route that was known as Castleman's Corkscrew. The branch towards Lymington Pier heads away to the right alongside the signal box in the background. *Colour Rail*

Having taken this meandering parallel inland route ourselves, we arrive at West Moors just in time to meet up with Standard Class 4MT Mogul, 76068 passing through. Note the child's scooter and a large box of Player's Cigarettes awaiting passage on the next stopping train on 4 July 1959. *Colour Rail*

A delightful view from August 1963 across the Dorset countryside as Class M7, 30667 heads away from Corfe Castle on the Swanage branch. *Colour Rail*

The Class M7s may have gone, but regular branch line steam could still be found here at Swanage on 4 September 1966, as Ivatt Class 2MTs and Standard Class 4MTs in both 2-6-4T and 2-6-0 forms, along with the Class 3MT 2-6-2T varieties hung on until replaced by DEMUs. *Colour Rail*

Succeeding the Class M7s here at Yeovil Town for a short while were the likes of this Collett Pannier Tank, 5416 seen shunting the Pen Mill shuttle on 21 April 1963. Meanwhile, in the station having just arrived with a local service an un-rebuilt Bulleid Pacific stands alongside the shed yards. *Rail Photoprints*

The three surviving Adams Radial Tanks drew many cameramen here to the Lyme Regis branch through the years before they were replaced briefly by Ivatt Class 2MTs, who in turn gave way to DMUs and then to complete closure. Happier times for these travellers on a warm and sunny 16 August 1959, with 30582 on duty just now and running around. *Colour Rail*

Opposite: There was often plenty of time to enjoy one's working life back in those halcyon days, as both the driver and the signalman at Sidmouth take a moment to watch our cameraman and get themselves into the picture too, during August 1959. As they are also seen running around their branch line train with Ivatt Class 2MT, 41307 on what was a 72A Exmouth Junction duty. *Rail Photoprints*

Also to be found on branch line duties were some of 72A Exmouth Junction's allocation of Standard Class 3MTs, such as the horribly filthy 82023, sorting itself out with this rake of coaches at Halwill Junction on 11 October 1962. This is where the Okehampton to Bude line met with lines from Launceston and Barnstaple Junction. *Colour Rail*

The terminus here at Bude was reached by the LSWR in 1898, deep into territory that the rival GWR saw as their own. Aside from local passenger traffic such as this example with Maunsell N Class, 31409 there was also a daily direct connection to Waterloo, with a coach running through as part of the multi-portioned Atlantic Coast Express for the benefit of holidaymakers, before we all discovered air travel for our holidays. Sadly this section of the Withered Arm here to serve Bude, was to close on 3 October 1966. *Colour Rail*

Opposite: This young fireman has most likely donned his jacket to try and protect him from getting wet, as he struggles to sort out the hose and into the tanks of Class O2, 30193 during the stop at Calstock on 6 May 1961. Meanwhile, his driver hangs onto the chain ready to start the water flowing from the tank above as they work the Callington branch from Bere Alston.
Colour Rail

Passengers and the fireman alike take this chance to enjoy a leisurely run through the North Cornwall countryside on a pleasant spring day, near Egloskerry on the Padstow branch. Sixty-six of these Drummond Class T9s came into British Railway's ownership in 1948, however by 19 April 1960, their numbers had dwindled to just thirteen examples including 30715.
Colour Rail

This Class T9 stands at Camelford as a porter assists passengers off this Okehampton to Padstow service on 5 July 1960, already standing outside the station the local parcel delivery van waits to see what has just arrived too. *Rail Photoprints*

Wadebridge station and goods yards still appeared prosperous when visited on 27 July 1963, as we see 34002 Salisbury heading away with a local, leaving behind a Collett Pannier Tank with what was most likely a service from Bodmin. *Colour Rail*

We cannot come this far into Cornwall without seeking out one of the three Beattie Well Tanks that were based at Wadebridge for working the Wenford Bridge line. We find today's footplate crew having a tea break at Dunmere Junction with 30587 on 14 October 1960. Next, we head back through Wadebridge and onwards to meet the sea here at Padstow, where one of Dugald Drummond's graceful Class T9s is involved with a little shunting of stock. *Both: Colour Rail*

It's tragic to think that when Class T9, 30715 was seen shunting at Padstow on 27 June 1961, she was just over week from being posted as withdrawn, and worse still she was cut up at Eastleigh Works within six weeks of this photograph, as the cutters got straight to work clearing the congested lines of withdrawn locomotives littering the works at this time. *Rail Online*

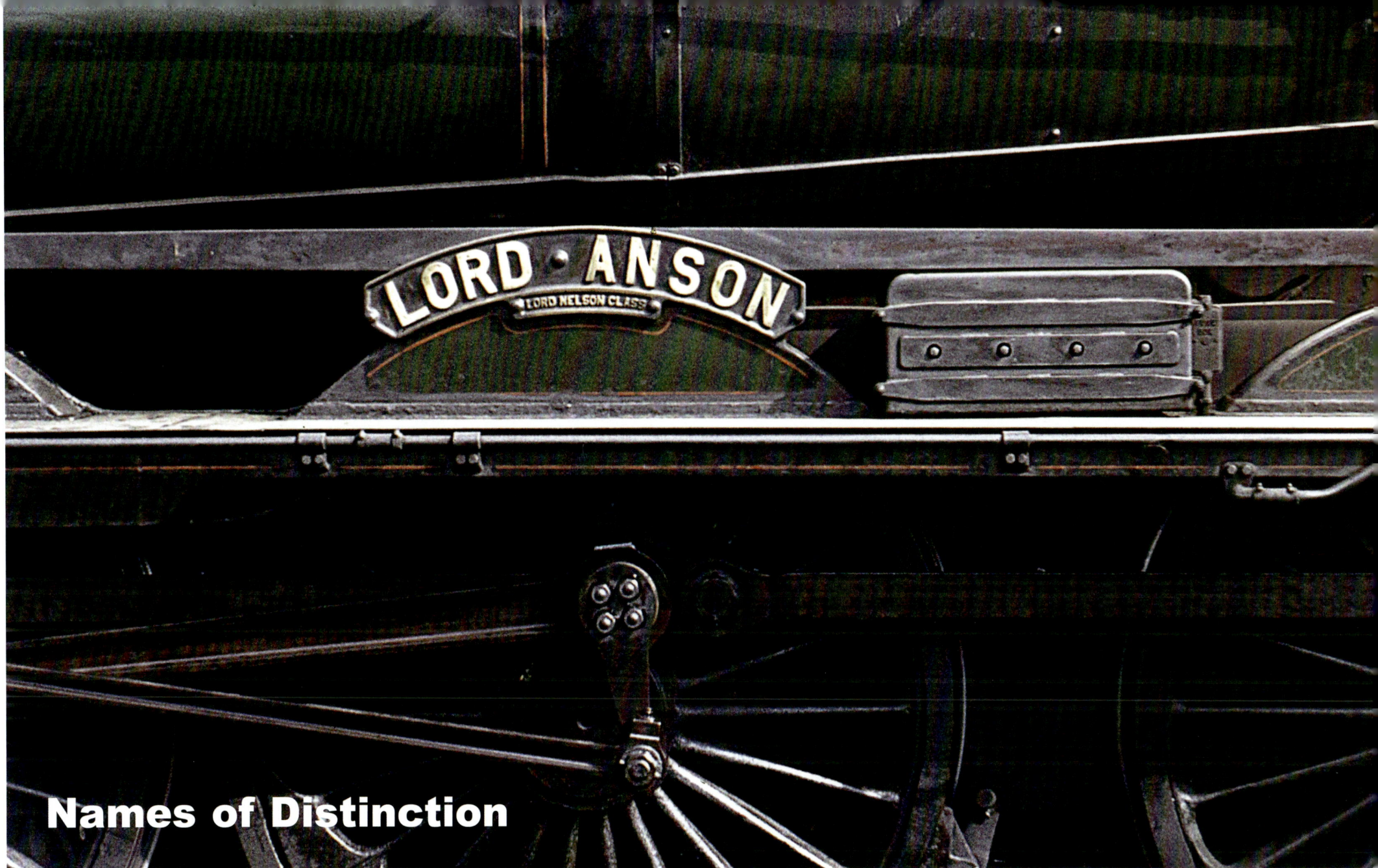

Names of Distinction

With the AWS box now fitted alongside we can still enjoy the nameplates fitted to 30861 Lord Anson. He is best remembered for his exploits while England was at war with Spain in 1740. He led a squadron of eight ships on a mission to disrupt or capture Spain's Pacific possessions. He returned home in 1744 by way of China and thus completed a circumnavigation of the globe. Although the voyage was notable for the capture of an Acapulco galleon there were horrific losses to disease with only 188 men of the original 1,854 surviving. *Colour Rail*

Of the sixteen locomotives within this Maunsell designed class of 4-6-0s only the class leader 30850 Lord Nelson, omitted the class name within the nameplate. The name for 30862 commemorates Lord Collingwood's connection with Lord Nelson as his second in command at the Battle of Trafalgar with notoriety, both as master of his ship the Royal Sovereign and by taking command of the battle on the death of Nelson. Following Trafalgar, he was awarded a peerage but died at sea in 1810 and was later buried in St. Paul's Cathedral. *Both: Colour Rail*

To discover the background to Sir Brian within the Arthurian legends is to recall many other Class N15 names too. Sir Brian was the brother of Sir Meliot de Logres and an enemy of King Arthur, as such he imprisoned both knights and ladies, including Sir Gawain, as a form of entertainment. That is until Sir Lancelot forced him to release them, and took the castle as his own, renaming it as Joyous Gard. Afterwards, Sir Brian joined forces with a disgruntled Sir Kay and invaded Britain from France while King Arthur was on a pilgrimage. They pillaged the countryside and marched on Carlisle, but were defeated by Sir Gawain and Sir Lancelot. Sir Brian was wounded but, upon his recovery, he became involved with an invasion of Scotland, when he was finally killed in battle by Sir Lancelot. *Colour Rail*

Nine of Marsh's Class H1 and H2 Atlantics joined British Railways service in 1948, the last to survive in traffic was 32424 Beachy Head, which was withdrawn in April 1958. They all bore names of notable South Coast landmarks. *Colour Rail*

The seven locomotives of the N15X class of 4-6-0s rebuilt by Maunsell that British Railways inherited in 1948, were all except 32333 named after locomotive engineers, such as Beattie which was awarded to 32331, it was also the last to remain in service until July 1957. The class bore the name Remembrance which was the name of 32333 in respect of the men of the LBSCR who lost their lives in the First World War. *Colour Rail*

We have already taken a wider look at the forty locomotives making up Maunsell's Schools Class or as it was officially classified as V Class. They were all named after some of the country's public schools, such as 30925 Cheltenham and 30910 Merchant Taylors. Originally 30923 carried the name of Uppingham for its first few months in traffic until August 1934, when it became Bradfield. *Both: Colour Rail*

An unfortunate mistake occurred in September 1960, when both 34058 Sir Frederick Pile and 34068 Kenley were undergoing overhauls together within Eastleigh Works. The nameplates and badges had all been removed and when they were refitted to the locomotives, they were unfortunately mixed up. Thus the RAF insignia is seen fitted to 34058 Sir Frederick Pile here, whereas his coat of arms was inadvertently refitted to 34068 Kenley, this is how they remained until withdrawn. *Colour Rail*

Of the sixty-six West Country Pacifics, thirty-six of them including 34100 Appledore carried their names without any form of shields as shown here, unlike 34017 Ilfracombe, both of these examples are in their rebuilt condition with additional backplates.
Photos: Colour Rail & Rail Online

Previous page: Both 34050 Royal Observer Corps with its Long Service Medal Ribbon and 34067 Tangmere seen here gained further cab side embellishments under British Railways. *Colour Rail*

The impressively large three-piece nameplates fitted to the Merchant Navy Class in their original guise were bolted direct to the casing, with the flags always showing to show the wind flowing correctly when facing forward, as here on 35013 Blue Funnel on 27 March 1954. *Colour Rail*

When the Merchant Navy class were rebuilt, to transfer the original nameplates to their new curved boiler casings, a special supporting cradle was fitted as we can see from the fixing bolts around the perimeter here of 35030 Elder-Dempster Lines. *Colour Rail*

Opposite: On 16 August 1964, the Warwickshire Railway Society ran their Swindon & Eastleigh Railtour involving visits to both railway works. This was hauled throughout by the world-famous 4472 Flying Scotsman, we see her at Salisbury during a shunting manoeuvre just as a Bulleid Pacific appears. *Strathwood Library Collection*

Southern Specials

Although it was frowned upon then too, we can see that enthusiasts trespassing upon the railway, especially to photograph and observe specials was commonplace in the age of steam. Both of these shots depict two of the nine legs that made up the L.C.G.B.'s Hayling Farewell tour on 3 November 1963. The platforms are crowded at Fratton as one of Urie's Class S15s come off the tour in favour of 34088 213 Squadron who will take up the next leg. Then opposite we join all of those trespassing upon the lineside to enjoy 32636 leading with 36270 in the rear as the two Terriers top and tail the special from Havant to Hayling Island. *Both: Colour Rail*

The R.C.T.S. and the Stephenson Locomotive Society combined to run The South Western Suburban Railtour using two of the Beattie Well Tanks 30585 and 30587. These were brought up from Cornwall specifically for this tour before they were to be sent to Eastleigh Works for scrapping. We see the pair on the 2 December 1962, passing Wimbledon just before 11.30 am on their way to Hampton Court. The tour was so popular that a rerun was arranged which took place a fortnight later. After which all three of these Class 0298 Well Tanks were withdrawn, but in the end it was 30586, the only one not to take part in these tours that was cut up, the other two headed for preservation. Also involved in both tours was this Urie Class H16, 30517 from 70B Feltham. All five of the class had been withdrawn during November, however, 30517 was given a short reprieve and it was bulled up to run both specials on the legs from Wimbledon Yard to Chessington and return. We see her in Wimbledon's yard awaiting the return of the Well Tanks so she can head for Chessington on the first tour on 2 December. *Both: Colour Rail*

Another tour around the former LSWR suburban network on 19 March 1961, brought this Adams Radial Tank 30582 here to Windsor & Eton Riverside during the mid-afternoon thanks to the Railway Enthusiasts Club. *Colour Rail*

On 7 June 1958, an ex-works push-pull set was used along with Class M7, 30107 for the Railway Enthusiast Club's South Dorset Railtour which we pick up at Dorchester West. *Colour Rail*

The Midhurst Belle tour of 18 October 1964, started from Waterloo behind Maunsell Class S15, 30839 which is seen near Bagshot on this glorious morning heading for Woking to hand over to USA Class, 30064 which then took over for the next leg. This is where we see it leaving Christ's Hospital just over seventy miles into this one hundred and ninety-two-mile tour, which also employed Q Class 30530 and 35007 Aberdeen Commonwealth as well. *Both: Colour Rail*

The L.C.G.B. offered their Solent Limited tour on 30 April 1961, which included a visit to Eastleigh Works along with two hundred and thirty-three miles of travel including seven locomotives. Up first was Lord Nelson, 30856 Lord St. Vincent which brought them here to Portsmouth Harbour from Waterloo.

Drummond Class T9, 30117 then gets us as far as Fareham for the next changeover where we see Class E1, 32694 and Class O2 30200 waiting about to take on the next leg. *Both: Colour Rail*

For the Railway Enthusiast Club's East Kent Railway tour on 23 May 1959, it was a much more modest affair just utilising Class O1, 31258 for the entire run to visit this light railway. Our view shows the special at Shepherds Well with an empty van between the tender and the tour's two coaches to help distribute the weight and to help with clearance on such tight curves. *Colour Rail*

Another well-subscribed L.C.G.B. railtour was held on Sunday 24 June 1962, which started out from Waterloo behind the preserved Class T9, 120. Taking a circuitous route they arrived here at Bognor Regis mid-afternoon behind K Class 32353, which was turned on the old shed's turntable after arrival from Pulborough before taking the tour onwards to Haywards Heath. *Colour Rail*

On this same L.C.G.B. tour, we get to enjoy Class M7, 30055 coming off the train at Rotherfield having double-headed us from Eastbourne to leave the preserved Class T9 then in sole charge for the run back to Waterloo. Earlier in the day the participants enjoyed further double-heading from Horsham to here at Midhurst and back to Pulborough behind Class E6, 32417 and Class E4, 32503. *Both: Colour Rail*

The Southern Region's, U Class 31639 found itself on a number of rail tours in the mid-sixties, with four outings alone in the first three months of 1966. One of which brought it here to Fareham on 9 January 1966, as part of the S15 Commemorative Railtour which starred 30837 and also used USA Class, 30073 for the shunt in and out of Eastleigh Works. *Colour Rail*

Opposite: Likewise, 34051 Winston Churchill found itself booked for both runnings of the L.C.G.B.'s Wessex Downsman tours which was run twice due to the high level of demand on 4 April and again on 2 May 1965. This is the first run awaiting departure from Bournemouth West. *Strathwood Library Collection*

Opposite: Ivatt Class 2MT, 41298 slowly inches its way past all the cars parked along the Weymouth Quay branch with the L.C.G.B.'s Green Arrow Railtour on 3 July 1966. *Rail Photoprints*

While the tour participants were visiting Eastleigh Works as mentioned on page 65, 4472 Flying Scotsman took her leave for servicing here in the shed yard on 18 August 1964. *Rail Online*

Shed & Works Visits

Although she had been officially withdrawn in November 1963 after the closure of the Hayling Island branch, 32636 was put back into steam for testing at Eastleigh in early 1964 before being sold to the Bluebell Railway for £750. *Colour Rail*

Strangely Basingstoke's Drummond 700 Class, 30698 is showing a 70B Feltham shed code in this view of her on what was supposed to be her home shed of 70D Basingstoke during 1961, she also carries special brackets to attach the larger snow ploughs for working 'over the Alps' as the Mid-Hants route was known to be some winters. *Colour Rail*

Two visits to Brighton shed in connection with a couple of enthusiast's specials, firstly on 15 September 1963, as this Terrier keeps a close watch over the preserved duo of the Caledonian Railway's 123 and the LSWR's 120. Almost a year beforehand another visit on 7 October 1962, saw Class E6, 32418 quenching its thirst while also on rail tour duty. *Both: Colour Rail*

Opposite: A nice view to show all of the equipment added to those motor-fitted Drummond Class M7s such as Eastleigh's 30480 sitting quietly in the works yard around 1962. *Colour Rail*

One of the earlier 0-4-4Ts for the LSWR was this Adams designed Class O2, 30229 on shed at Eastleigh on 18 April 1960, with less than a year's life left in this relic from 1894. *Colour Rail*

In an attempt to replace their ageing collection of 0-4-4Ts in the late fifties, a reasonable number of Collett's Pannier Tanks were drafted onto the Southern Region. Among their number, was 4666 which had already been on the region since October 1959, and is seen in the shed yard at Barnstaple Junction on 18 July 1963, as she had just been re-allocated here a few weeks beforehand and was yet to receive her new shed plate. *Rail Online*

Whereas, this ex-LSWR Class S15 designed by Urie and built here at Eastleigh in December 1912, was always a long-standing faithful servant to the Southern Region as a resident of 70B Feltham from nationalization until withdrawn on 16 November 1963. This was not so long after this photograph was taken of her on shed at Eastleigh. She then lent further employment to the region's staff in January the following year to cut her up in the works yard. *Colour Rail*

A senior man lends a hand to trim the coal in the tender of Lord Nelson Class, 30852 Sir Walter Raleigh from 71A Eastleigh shed, out in the yard by the turntable at Bournemouth on 21 February 1960. *Colour Rail*

Opposite: An even coat of grime flattens the paintwork of another of Maunsell's 4-6-0s in the shape of his version of the S15 Class, 30842 complete with an eight-wheel tender sunning itself in the shed yard at Yeovil around 1962. *Colour Rail*

Another perhaps everyday, less glamorous view across the shed yard at 75A Brighton from the overlooking roadway, with eleven locomotive classes to be seen when taken on 6 August 1961. *Colour Rail*

When the demise came for King Arthur Class 4-6-0, 30795 Sir Dinadan seen here at Easteligh's shed on 18 September 1960, it was swift as she was reported as withdrawn officially the week ending 4 August 1962, in reality, she had already been cut up here at Eastleigh about the same time! *Colour Rail*

Close inspection shows that the tender of this rebuilt Battle of Britain, 34087 145 Squadron has taken a gouge through some careless movements within the close confines of a yard somewhere, fortunately not deep enough to cause a water leak when it was viewed on shed at Bournemouth on 15 September 1963. *Colour Rail*

Opposite: The extended smoke deflectors fitted to the un-rebuilt West Country 34006 Bude in 1948 show up straight away in this 4 August 1966 scene taken at Nine Elms. Two others were likewise treated to these longer deflectors, 34004 and 34005, but they lost theirs when they were rebuilt, just leaving 34006 Bude in this condition until withdrawn on 19 March 1967. *Colour Rail*

The clean powerful lines of Lord Nelson Class, 30854 Howard of Effingham in this late fifties view at Eastleigh, shows no signs of her earlier battering when she was derailed at speed and careered down an embankment at nearby Shawford in 1952. *Colour Rail*

Opposite: These two chaps look really too young to already be passed cleaners as they move this Maunsell W Class along the shed's side roads at 70B Feltham on 23 June 1963. To keep the locomotive in traffic some fairly basic welding repairs have been made to her water tanks to patch them up, this perhaps helped to keep her going until withdrawn on 5 January six months later. *Colour Rail*

Looking west from the top of the Feltham coaler in the winter of 1961, the diesel invasion for working the expansive hump yard now has five diesel shunters on shed with another attending the wagon repair shops to the right. Among the usual Sunday suspects on shed, there is a Pannier Tank most likely in from Nine Elms, although Feltham did have a couple for a short while too. *Rail Photoprints*

Opposite: Somehow the smaller transfer applied to the tender of 33027 of the British Railways emblem looks out of scale and lost on these powerful Bulleid Q1 Class 0-6-0s in this view taken in the shed yard at Nine Elms on 10 October 1964. *Colour Rail*

Opposite: The extra cab side embellishment fitted to Battle of Britain Class, 34067 Tangmere shows up again in this view from 27 July 1963, as she takes a spin on the turntable which gave access to the many shed roads here at Nine Elms. *Rail Online*

Another elevated view across the shed yard at 75A Brighton from 14 September 1959, looking out towards the viaduct carrying the line towards Lewes with a four-car rake of EMUs. Check out whats on shed today and see if you can spot the Stanier Class 8F and Black Five? *Colour Rail*

A mid-sixties view on shed at Salisbury of 34057 Biggin Hill in un-rebuilt form reminds us of their tendency to suffer from lagging fires. As the repainting, although smart around her casing has omitted the lining over the damaged area. *Colour Rail*

No such firey foibles to afflict this Maunsell Class D1, 31739 being turned at Ashford around 1961 which was to be her last year in traffic before being cut up in the adjoining works during January 1962. *Colour Rail*

Opposite: The rims of the wheels on both the Standard Class 4MT 75069, and the Bulleid Class Q1, 33005 show just how quickly a patina of rust forms on them, as they stand out in the winter drizzle with both locomotives in steam waiting to go off shed from Stewarts Lane on 25 February 1961. *Colour Rail*

Rebuilt West Country, 34096 Trevone stands on the ash disposal road at Nine Elms during May 1964. Those peculiar concrete mounds were the foundations for the original LSWR coal stage sited here before the Southern Railway installed their new ferroconcrete construction known locally as 'the cenotaph'. *Colour Rail*

The powerful no-nonsense lines of Urie's Class H16, 4-6-2T is well portrayed here from the road bridge that gave access to both the works and the engine sheds at Eastleigh during 1961. *Colour Rail*

Keeping a respectful distance in the queue for coal at Salisbury shed on 15 September 1962, the fireman of Standard Class 4MT Mogul, 76055 keeps a watch on proceedings. *Colour Rail*

Oliver Bulleid's strides for innovation and development is clear in these two views taken at Eastleigh's works, firstly in 1950 with the recently applied blue livery to his Merchant Navy Pacific, 35017 Belgian Marine. Perhaps more notably is his sole actual working prototype for his Leader Class, 36001 as she awaits final painting before going out on proper testing during 1949. *Both: Colour Rail*

Eastleigh Works has just carried out an overhaul on behalf of Folkestone Junction shed to one of their panniers used for banking heavy trains up from the harbour branch. Here 4626 awaits delivery back home to the Eastern Section on 4 March 1961. That October she would head west once again to join the allocation at 72B Salisbury next. *Colour Rail*

Opposite: The bell finally tolled for 70B Feltham's Drummond 700 Class 30346, during November 1962. In this view from around this time out in the shed yard here, she has already lost her smokebox numberplate and her 1897 built Dubs works plates too, however, she still has a full load of coal to be removed before scrapping, or was she worked to Eastleigh in steam? *Colour Rail*

Feltham shed's scrap line holds twelve locomotives in this view from 8 March 1964, this includes four Q1s, five S15s, and one each of Classes H16, W and M7. The lead engine in this string, 33003 would head to King's of Norwich that October to be scrapped there the following spring. *Colour Rail*

Isle of Wight Sunset

We start our visit to the railway across the Solent here at Mill Hill on the former Isle of Wight Central Railway's station on the Cowes line. Where on 12 August 1965, business still looks prosperous from a mix of locals and holidaymakers alike to join this service, headed by W22 Brading working bunker first from Cowes. A similar service was recorded closeby on 18 September the same year, headed by W20 Shanklin on this occasion. *Both: Colour Rail*

This recently released from Ryde Works, Stroudley Class E1, has the task today of shunting Shanklin's Gas Works sidings during June 1954. Sadly W2 Yarmouth would be the first of the four Class E1s to be withdrawn by British Railways on the island, in September 1956. *Colour Rail*

Of the twenty-three Adams Class O2s to work the island's services during the same era, W20 Shanklin was among the last ten to remain in traffic for the final passenger workings on 31 December 1966. We catch her near Wroxall on 18 September 1965, with an evening service just before sunset. *Colour Rail*

This well loaded six-coach service forces W22 Brading into a little hard working at Smallbrook Junction in June 1965. This also helps to explain why the Isle of Wight Class O2s had extended coal bunkers as we see W29 Alverstone taking water on 18 September the same season during a stop at Newport. *Both: Colour Rail*

A bright and sunny clear morning dawns on the last day for passenger services to be steam hauled on 31 December 1966, and we have a good turn out at Ryde shed to witness the preparations for the locomotives to be tasked with running today's enthusiast specials and service trains. We can also see the artist David Shepherd hastily doing his best with his sketches and colour notes at his easel to record the moment too.

A belated attempt at cleaning up W14 Fishbourne is being made after she has been adorned with a wreath and a discrete headboard to mark the day. Regular service trains were still being run, but the bulk of the enthusiasts would arrive here thanks to an L.C.G.B. special run from Waterloo behind Standard Class 5MTs 73065 and 73043. They made a connection with the ferry MV Southsea arriving just before 11.00 on the island. Here their waiting double-headed special behind W24 Calbourne and W31 Chale would take them from Ryde Pierhead to Shanklin and a return to Ryde Pierhead once more in time to meet the ferry MV Brading for their run back to London behind 34013 Okehampton. *Both: Colour Rail*

Also bearing another final day headboard along with some half-hearted cleaning W17 complete with makeshift replacement Seaview nameplates comes past the shed yard at Ryde St. Johns also on 31 December 1966. *Colour Rail*

We take our leave from the island with this view of W35 Freshwater coming off Ryde Pier with the 19.19 bound for Shanklin one evening in September 1966. *Colour Rail*

There is no fear of 75C Norwood Junction's 31919 running out of coal for this shift, as the Maunsell W Class takes up a spot of gentle shunting at Oxted on 18 May 1963. There seems to be an awful lot of mailbags further down the platform here at Gravesend Central on 6 April 1961, as the crew of this H Class, 31512 from 74D Tonbridge take a break from their Allhallows branch duties for a spell. The shed code for Tonbridge incidentally changed from 74D to 73J on 13 October 1958, but nobody has bothered to change the plate on the engine so far, as she was withdrawn a couple of months later its doubtful anyone ever did. *Both: Colour Rail*

The fireman of this Urie Class S15, 30502 from 70B Feltham keeps an eye out for one of the Broad Street to Richmond EMUs to pass, in order that they can follow it back to rejoin the Southern Region themselves near Kew Bridge after picking up a freight at nearby Willesden and heading for Feltham's busy marshalling yard. *Colour Rail*

Another Standard Class 4MT Mogul can be seen shunting the yard at Wareham as 76012 arrives with a stopper during June 1966. *Colour Rail*

The flyover at Worting Junction where the Salisbury and Bournemouth lines part south of Basingstoke allows continued high speed running, as here with 30859 Lord Hood approaching us fast heading for Winchester and the Bournemouth route around 1960. *Colour Rail*

Opposite: As part of the electrification scheme for the Kent Coast, the Southern Region invested in similar improvements for higher speed running here through St. Mary Cray, where 30796 Sir Dodinas le Savage sweeps by on 26 March 1959, with the 11.35 Victoria to Ramsgate. *Rail Photoprints*

The shunting work today is spilling into the platform roads here at Tunbridge Wells West for this Wainwright designed C Class 31590, with an interesting pair of brake vans in the mix during October 1957. *Colour Rail*

The staggered platforms at Raynes Park have always been an attraction for cameramen to take photographs of both up and down expresses, as here with 34052 Lord Dowding on the down fast on 19 October 1963. *Colour Rail*

Having most likely come down from Nine Elms for a Waterloo departure ahead of time, doubleheaded with another light-engine in order to minimize line occupation at this busy terminus. This means, 34039 Boscastle is now forced to wait in the parcels bay out of harm's way on 8 July 1962, until the Waterloo signalmen are ready for her. Just after nationalization, the Southern Region employed both M7 and E4 tanks from Nine Elms shed as the main station pilots and to work ecs to and from Waterloo to here at Clapham Junction. The yard here was sandwiched between the Windsor lines and the Bournemouth mainline. Several Pannier Tanks arrived and took over briefly in the early sixties, however, the Nine Elms men disliked them, so in turn, a mix of Ivatt Class 2MTs, Standard Class 4MTs and Standard Class 3MTs such as 82018 became the norm as here on 20 September 1965. *Both: Colour Rail*

132

Opposite: This Wainwright H Class is making a brief stop at Hever a former LBSCR station with a push/pull set on 31 May 1963, as we can see the station was still lit by oil lamps at this time. *Colour Rail*

Some rather nice town's-gas fed swan neck lamps were still to be found in place at Weymouth on 21 February 1966, as Merchant Navy Class, 35027 Port Line awaits departure. *Colour Rail*

Electric lighting was just being installed to illuminate the platforms properly for passengers here at Groombridge on 15 June 1957. The elegant 4-4-0, 31470 which the young lad has his eye upon was first built at Ashford Works in August 1906, but was one of twenty D Class engines that were rebuilt between 1921 – 1927 to become Maunsell's Class D1s. *Colour Rail*

Richard Edward Lloyd Maunsell CBE held the post of the chief mechanical engineer of the South Eastern and Chatham Railway from 1913 until the 1923 Grouping and then the post of CME for the Southern Railway until succeeded in 1937 by Bulleid. His influence on the Southern was felt for a long time afterwards with both the N Class 31869 on the freight and the rake of 2-BIL EMUs heading away from us here at Ash on 21 April 1956. *Colour Rail*

Opposite: Perhaps they are discussing the impending doom of 30861 Lord Anson by the water crane at Salisbury on 2 September 1962, as she went into Eastleigh Works soon afterwards and was withdrawn on 6 October. *Colour Rail*

We wonder if there is anyone checking to see how tight the clearances are to the parked cars as Standard Class 5MT, 73169 from 70D Eastleigh shunts the yard at Fleet on 15 January 1965. *Colour Rail*

Opposite: On 26 March 1964, all appeared well here at Bailey Gate on the former Somerset & Dorset Joint Railway's route through the Mendips, as Standard Class 5MT, 73049 made its stop to discharge a good trolley full of baskets and to pick up a passenger or two perhaps. The station served the large United Dairies Cheese Factory seen in the background as well as the village of Sturminster Marshall after whom it was originally named when opened in 1860, however, it was renamed in 1863 after a local farm to avoid confusion with another station on the same line at Sturminster Newton. *Colour Rail*

Having been given the road towards Andover and Salisbury at Worting Junction on 25 August 1962, this Urie Class S15 starts to accelerate once more at the head of its stopping train. Notice how the railway workmen's cottages to the left have a footpath that leads straight along the line from their gardens. *Colour Rail*

Having been checked previously the somewhat filthy 35026 Lamport & Holt Line has been given the double peg again as she runs through Winchfield with the Bournemouth Belle on 1 August 1965. *Strathwood Library Collection*

Now here is an interesting one for modellers as 34045 Ottery St. Mary runs tender first over the River Stour hauling a two-coach push/pull set and a van as a fill-in turn on 12 October 1963, at Wimbourne. *Colour Rail*

A gentleman out walking his dog pauses to admire the passing of the down Bournemouth Belle near Worting Junction, hauled this morning by 34071 601 Squadron on 9 March 1966.
Strathwood Library Collection

Considering the date, 35013 Blue Funnel looks respectable enough as she sets off from her Basingstoke stop on 29 March 1967. *Gilroy A. Kerr*

Passing the interesting signal box and the watchful eyes of the signalman above on 23 May 1959, 34078 222 Squadron negotiates Kearsney Loop Junction. *Colour Rail*

KEARSNEY LOOP JUNCTION

The famous Tor overlooks this busy scene at Glastonbury & Street in January 1966 as the driver exchanges the tokens with the signalman and a reasonable number of passengers appear to be present a short while before closure on 7 March 1966. *Colour Rail*

Opposite: Likewise, passenger numbers look good at Wareham on 7 August 1963, on both the up and down platforms. Compare the gable ends of the platform canopies for embellishment differences with those opposite. *Colour Rail*

A brief look back to passing times at Eastleigh station as 6923 Croxteth Hall has pulled in during May 1964 with an inter-regional job from Oxford. *Colour Rail*

Opposite: A relief crew await their train as 73171 arrives at Eastleigh on 3 September 1966, those shiny shoes of the fireman do not look like railway issue! *Gilroy A. Kerr*

A perhaps unlikely shunter of passenger stock at Eastleigh in 1955 was the nicely cleaned 7906 Fron Hall from 81D Reading. *Colour Rail*

Opposite: Another view of 30861 Lord Anson waiting alongside the water crane at Salisbury on 2 September 1962, it was customary for the fireman before being relieved to help shovel forward coal in the tender with the new fireman, as the two drivers topped up the tender with water and exchanged words about their locomotive. Hence the spare shovels kept handy in the drain funnel from the water crane in front of us. *Colour Rail*

With his day's work completed this footplateman climbs the platform ramp into Templecombe Lower station having booked off duty at the shed behind, the bridge above him carries the former LSWR mainline to the West Country in this scene from November 1964. *Colour Rail*

Opposite: We can see how the Nine Elms cleaners have cheated when wiping over the boiler of this Merchant Navy, by missing out what they think their 'guv'nor' might not see from down at ground level. Although in September 1962, 35029 Ellerman Lines still makes an impressive sight passing the redundant wartime defences alongside the mainline at Winchfield. *Colour Rail*

Feltham's Maunsell W Class, 31917 puts in another appearance with its patched-up side tanks during 1963. Having a day out around Clapham Junctions' busy carriage cleaning and storage yard this time, with perhaps the odd ecs working to and from Waterloo thrown in for good measure during the shift as required. *Colour Rail*

Opposite: This un-rebuilt Bulleid Pacific was a regular on the Somerset & Dorset for many years, therefore it was no real surprise for 34043 Combe Martin to turn up here at Midford with a down local in July 1963. *Colour Rail*

There appears to be a spot of trouble hooking Standard Class 3MT, 82029 back onto the push/pull set for the Swanage branch here at Wareham during the summer of 1964, during her time based out of 70F Bournemouth. *Colour Rail*

It looks like this 1895 built Class R1, has performed a few banking turns already on this day in 1954 judging by the amount of coal left in her bunker, as she waits to go again from Folkestone Harbour up the 1 in 30 towards the junction with the mainline. *Colour Rail*

As the last of the Merchant Navy's to be rebuilt 35028 Clan Line became unique as the only one of her class to get the later crest applied to her tender before her rebuild in the late summer of 1959. This view of her on the Golden Arrow at Abbotscliffe is thought to date from that last summer of the fifties in her original guise. *Colour Rail*

Opposite: The unfortunate 34084, 253 Squadron gives us an unusual view of her following an accident at Hither Green 20 February 1960. After running gently through a stop block with a freight train from Dover to Bricklayers Arms she toppled down the embankment. Her recovery back up to track level to be hauled away for repairs took until 28 February. Meanwhile, as she took out a host of signalling wires in her fall from grace she caused chaos in the area for a while. *Roy Edgar Vincent/The Transport Treasury*

The chalked remarks adorning the smokebox of this Maunsell Class E1 4-4-0 might be a little hasty and premature when she was seen in the carriage sidings at Ramsgate on 18 June 1959, as she survived the Kent coast electrification process for a while longer until April 1961. This brought her stints at Salisbury, Nine Elms and Stewarts Lane sheds, before scrapping finally did take place in Ashford Works in June 1961. *Colour Rail*

We depart this volume with a splendidly evocative shot of 34044 Woolacombe racing through the snows of January 1962 from an overbridge in Bramshott Woods. *Colour Rail*